"*Women will have achieved true equality when men share with them the responsibility of bringing up the next generation.*"

For Laurel Eisner, unflagging in
her commitment to social justice
—D.R.

For Debbie, who loved all the
beautiful complexities of the law
—E.V.

Text copyright © 2020 by Doreen Rappaport
Illustrations copyright © 2020 by Eric Velasquez

First Edition, February 2020
10 9 8 7 6 5 4 3 2 1
FAC-029191-19319

Printed in Malaysia
This book is set in 15-pt Basilia/Linotype; 27-pt Goldenbook/Fontspring
Designed by Phil Buchanan

Library of Congress Cataloging-in-Publication Data

Names: Rappaport, Doreen, author. • Velasquez, Eric, illustrator.
Title: Ruth objects : the life of Ruth Bader Ginsburg / written by Doreen
    Rappaport ; illustrated by Eric Velasquez.
Description: First edition. • Los Angeles : Disney HYPERION, 2020.
Identifiers: LCCN 2018057036• ISBN 9781484747179 (hardcover) • ISBN
    1484747178 (hardcover)
Subjects: LCSH: Ginsburg, Ruth Bader—Juvenile literature. • Women
    judges—United States—Biography—Juvenile literature. • Jewish
    judges—United States—Biography—Juvenile literature. • Judges—United
    States—Biography—Juvenile literature. • United States. Supreme
    Court—Biography—Juvenile literature.
Classification: LCC KF8745.G56 R37 2020 • DDC 347.73/2634 [B] —dc23
LC record available at https://lccn.loc.gov/2018057036

Reinforced binding
Visit www.DisneyBooks.com

RUTH
OBJECTS

The Life of Ruth Bader Ginsburg

WRITTEN BY

Doreen Rappaport

ILLUSTRATED BY

Eric Velasquez

DISNEY • HYPERION

LOS ANGELES   NEW YORK

Ruth's mother, Celia, wanted to go to college,
but her family had only enough money
to pay for their eldest son to attend.
When Celia married, her husband
made her stop working as a bookkeeper.
He worried that people would think
he couldn't support his family.

Celia was determined that
Ruth's life would be different.
She taught Ruth to be independent
but not to snap back in anger,
and to stick to what she believed was right.

"My parents taught me to
love learning,
to care about people,
and to work hard
for whatever I wanted
or believed in."

Life in Brooklyn, New York,
offered many treats for Ruth—
bike riding, jumping rope, playing stoopball,
and zooming around on roller skates.

After school on Fridays, Ruth went
to the library and lugged five books home.
Jo March of *Little Women*
was one of Ruth's favorite fictional heroes.
Ruth also devoured the mysteries
solved by Nancy Drew, girl detective.

**"Nancy was an adventurer
who could think for herself,
and was the dominant person
in her relationship
with her boyfriend."**

Friday nights her family lit candles
for the start of the Jewish Sabbath.
In high school Ruth played the cello,
sold tickets for sporting events,
twirled a baton at football games,
wrote for the school newspaper,
and earned a place in the honor society.

But Ruth's teenage life was not carefree.
Her beloved mother was dying.
She passed away two days before Ruth
graduated from high school.

"My mother was the bravest and strongest person I have known."

In 1950 many colleges accepted no women.
Many limited the number of Jews, but
Cornell University gave Ruth a full scholarship.
Cornell, like most colleges then, had restrictive
rules for women, but not for men.
Women had to live on campus
and be in their rooms by 10:30 p.m.
They had to wear skirts at dinner.
Few women then objected.

Despite the rules, Cornell's teachers
had much to offer.
Author Vladimir Nabokov taught Ruth
to be exact in choosing words
to get her ideas across.

When a Cornell professor was
removed from his teaching duties
because he had once belonged to
a socialist organization,
Ruth was stunned.
Some lawyers helped people who had lost jobs
because of their political activities.
Their actions inspired Ruth.

"I got the idea that being a lawyer was a pretty good thing, because you could do something for your society."

Women then made up less than 3 percent
of all lawyers in the United States.

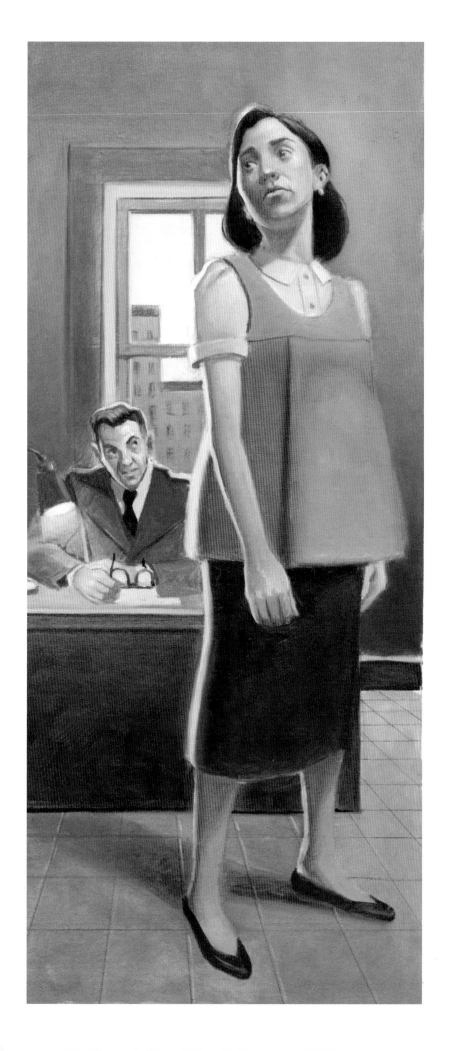

Martin Ginsburg thought Ruth
would make a great lawyer.
He was going to be one, too.

Marty was as outgoing as
Ruth was shy and quiet.
But they shared common values,
and their friendship grew into love.
When Ruth graduated from college,
they married.

When Marty was called up
for army service,
Ruth got a job with the government.
But when she told her boss that
she was going to have a baby,
she was demoted and
had to leave her job in
the ninth month of her pregnancy.

Ruth knew that being pregnant
would not stop her
from doing a good job, but that's what most
people thought then. Ruth also knew that
objecting would do no good.

"Marty always made me
feel I was better
than I thought I was,
that I could accomplish
whatever I sought."

Ruth graduated first in her class
and was accepted at Harvard Law School.
Ruth's class had nine women and 543 men.
Harvard treated men and
women differently, too.
There were no dormitories for women.
Women couldn't eat in the faculty club's main
dining room. There was a ladies' dining room.
The old periodicals room was closed to women.
Only one building where classes were held
had a women's bathroom.

At a dinner for the women law students,
the dean asked each woman
why she was taking a place
that could be held by a man.
Ruth explained,

"My husband is in the second-year class. I thought it important for a woman to understand her husband's work."

Of course, that wasn't her real reason.

Women of Ruth's generation
were encouraged to get married,
stay home, and cook, and clean,
and care for their families.
Men were supposed to earn the money.

Ruth and Marty had different ideas.
They shared household chores
and childcare.
Marty took up cooking because
Ruth was terrible at it.

When they were both in law school,
Marty became ill with a rare cancer.
He was too sick to go to class.
Ruth asked his friends to share
their notes from class lectures.
At night she typed the notes,
then did her own studying.
She often slept only two hours.
Marty recovered completely
and graduated on time.

"We survived that year
and learned that
nothing could happen that
we couldn't cope with."

Marty got a job in New York City and
Ruth transferred to Columbia Law School.
There were only twelve women
out of 280 in her class.

Ruth tied for first place in her graduating class,
but not one law firm interviewed her.

"Traditional law firms were just
beginning to hire Jews, but to be a
woman, a Jew, and a mother to boot,
that combination was a bit much."

Judges hire the top law graduates
to assist them as "law clerks,"
but not one judge offered Ruth a clerkship.
Finally, one of her professors
persuaded Judge Edmund L. Palmieri,
a judge who chose his clerks from
Columbia, to hire her.

"I worked harder than any
other law clerk.
Sometimes, I came in Saturdays,
even Sundays,
and brought work home."

Judge Palmieri could not have been
happier with Ruth's work.

In 1963 Ruth began teaching law
at Rutgers University in New Jersey.
She was paid less than male professors.
The dean explained to her that

"It was only fair to pay me modestly, because my husband had a very good job."

Ruth knew the dean
would never say that to a man.
She was being treated unequally,
but she knew objecting
might cost her the job.

Ruth became pregnant again.
She and Marty were joyful, but
she didn't tell anyone at school.
She wore loose clothing
so that no one would notice.
She didn't want to lose her job
as she had eleven years before,
when she was pregnant with her daughter.

Times were changing, though.
Blacks, Latinos, and Native Americans
were protesting for equal treatment before the law.
Women were meeting together,
sharing their lives, and demanding equal rights.

More women attended law school now.
Ruth's students asked her to teach
a course on women and the law.
Ruth found many laws that treated
men and women differently.

**"The 1787 notion of 'We the People'
left out the majority
of the adult population:
slaves, debtors, paupers,
Indians, and women.
The Constitution was a
document of governance
for and by white,
propertied adult males."**

It was time to challenge outmoded laws.
Ruth joined a lawsuit brought by
women professors at Rutgers
seeking equal pay with men.

The women won.

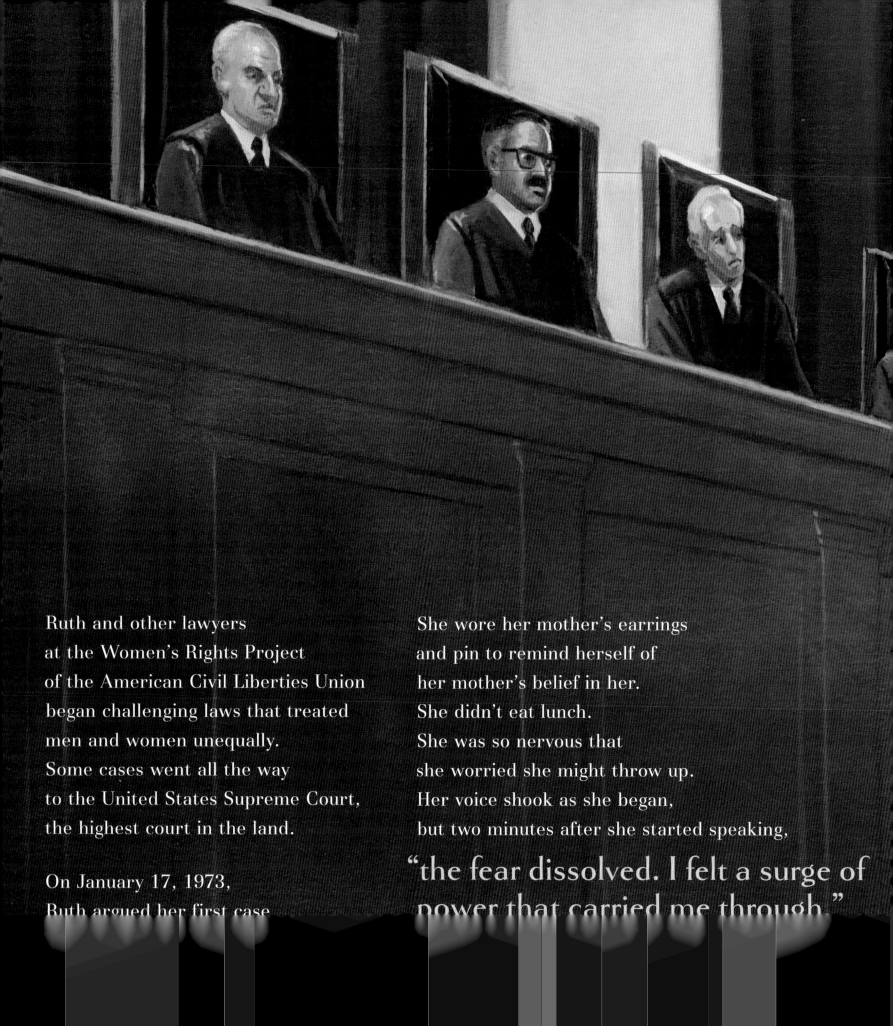

Ruth and other lawyers
at the Women's Rights Project
of the American Civil Liberties Union
began challenging laws that treated
men and women unequally.
Some cases went all the way
to the United States Supreme Court,
the highest court in the land.

On January 17, 1973,
Ruth argued her first case

She wore her mother's earrings
and pin to remind herself of
her mother's belief in her.
She didn't eat lunch.
She was so nervous that
she worried she might throw up.
Her voice shook as she began,
but two minutes after she started speaking,

"the fear dissolved. I felt a surge of
power that carried me through."

Ruth spoke for ten minutes
without any notes: She described how
air force lieutenant Sharron Frontiero
had applied for a housing allowance,
plus medical benefits for her husband.
Her husband was a college student.
She contributed most of the couple's support.

Her request to make her husband
a dependent was turned down.
Ruth reminded the justices that
military men received these benefits
for their wives,
no matter how much their wives earned.
This rule treated men and women
unequally before the law.

"I felt a sense of empowerment because I knew so much more about the case, the issue, than they did."

The justices ruled eight to one that the law was unconstitutional. Ruth and her team of lawyers celebrated their victory.

Ruth believed that inequality
harmed men as well as women.

When Stephen Wiesenfeld's wife died giving birth,
he was self-employed.
He wanted to care personally for his son
and work only part-time.
He needed money,
so he applied for survivor's benefits
based on his wife's payment of Social Security taxes.
He was turned down.

Ruth argued his case before the Supreme Court.
She pointed out to the nine male justices
that women received financial support
for childcare when their husbands died.
Men should receive the same support
if they assumed full care of their children.
The justices agreed.

"It is not women's liberation;
it is women's and men's liberation."

Over the next few years
Ruth argued six gender cases
before the Supreme Court
and won five of them.

In 1972 Ruth had been hired to teach
at Columbia Law School.
She found injustices there, too.
Twenty-five women housekeepers
were laid off.
Male janitors, doing the same work,
were not let go.

Ruth objected.
She told Columbia's vice president
in charge of business affairs that
this was a "grave and costly mistake."
The university reluctantly agreed
after a legal ruling stopped them
from firing the housekeepers.

Women workers at Columbia
had no medical coverage for childbirth.
Their pay and pensions
were lower than men's.
She filed lawsuits to change this.

The women won.

Ruth's reputation as a brilliant lawyer grew. In 1980 President Jimmy Carter appointed her a judge to the U.S. Court of Appeals for the District of Columbia Circuit. Marty took a new job in Washington, D.C., to be with Ruth.

In 1993 President Bill Clinton appointed her to the United States Supreme Court.

"I pray that I may be all that my mother would have been had she lived in an age when women could aspire and achieve and daughters are cherished as much as sons."

Now there were seven men and two women justices. Sandra Day O'Connor, the other woman on the Court, welcomed Ruth.

The two women didn't always agree on the answers to questions that came before the Court, but they both believed that women deserved equal protection under the law.

A case involving Virginia Military Institute
came before the Supreme Court.
This prestigious military school
refused to accept women,
insisting they were too weak to endure
the school's rigorous physical training.
The school also claimed that women could not
tolerate how upperclassmen would treat them.

Ruth believed that women should be able
to pursue all opportunities if qualified.
Excluding women violated
the equal protection clause of the
Fourteenth Amendment of the U.S. Constitution.

Justice O'Connor agreed.
So did five male justices.
The school was told to accept women or close.
It accepted women.

"If women are to be leaders
in life and in the military,
men have got to become
accustomed to taking
commands from women,
and men won't become
accustomed to that if
women aren't let in."

Lilly Ledbetter was the first
woman area manager in her factory.
After fifteen years of working,
she learned that she had been paid
thousands of dollars less than
the male managers.
Lilly objected,
and sued to get her back pay.
The case reached the Supreme Court.

The justices decided five to four against Lilly:
Five justices declared that workers
had to complain within 180 days
after the pay discrimination started.
Lilly had not done that.

When justices disagree on a ruling,
they often write a dissent explaining why.
On May 29, 2007, Ruth read her dissent
in court. She pointed out that it could
take much longer than 180 days
to find out that you were paid less
than your coworkers.
She suggested that Congress
rectify this injustice.

**"Sometimes one must
be forceful about saying how
wrong the Court's decision is."**

On January 29, 2009, Lilly watched
President Barack Obama sign
the Lilly Ledbetter Fair Pay Act,
which allowed workers to sue within
180 days of receiving any paycheck
unequal to the paycheck of
men doing the same job.
Ruth framed a copy of the law
to hang in her office.

Marty, who had a successful career,
took great joy in Ruth's work.
He read and critiqued her speeches and articles.
His gourmet meals delighted family and friends.
Ruth's law clerks loved the birthday cakes
he baked for them.
Their life together was filled with
the joy of family, travel, and music.

Most nights Marty had to telephone Ruth
to leave work and come home to eat.
After dinner, she went back to work.
He supported her during
her two bouts with cancer.

In 2010 Marty faced cancer again.
This time he did not survive.

"I do not have words adequate to describe my supersmart, exuberant, ever-loving spouse."

In 2006 Sandra Day O'Connor retired.
Ruth felt alone until 2009,
when Sonia Sotomayor was appointed to the Court.
Elena Kagan followed in 2010.

"Yes, women are here to stay.
And when I'm sometimes asked
when will there be enough
women on the Court,
and I respond when there are nine,
people are shocked.
But the Supreme Court has had
nine men for ever so long,
and nobody's ever raised
a question about that."

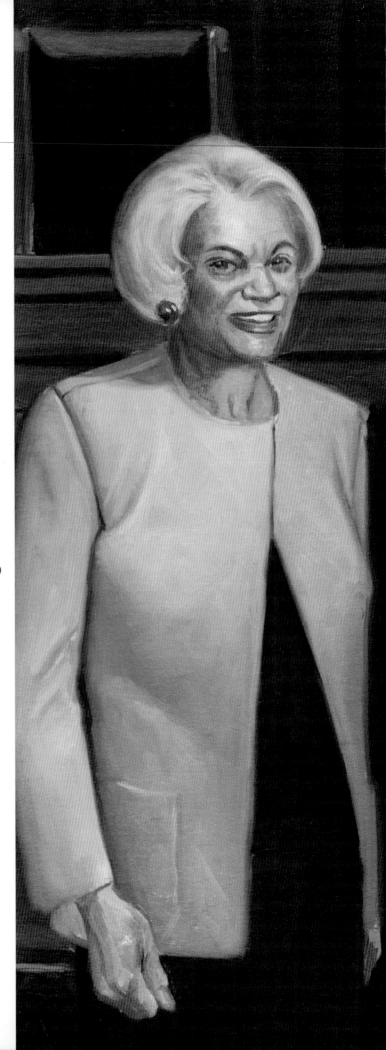

IMPORTANT DATES

March 15, 1933: Joan Ruth Bader is born to Celia Amster Bader and Nathan Bader.

June 6, 1934: Her older sister, Marilyn, dies at age six.

1938–1946: Ruth attends P.S. 238 in Brooklyn.

September 1946–June 1950: She attends James Madison High School in Brooklyn.

June 25, 1950: Ruth's mother dies.

1950–1954: She attends Cornell University. On June 23, 1954, she marries Martin Ginsburg.

1954–1956: Ruth and Marty live in Fort Sill, Oklahoma, while Marty serves in the army. On July 21, 1955, Jane Ginsburg is born.

1956–1958: Ruth attends Harvard Law School. Marty is one year ahead of her at Harvard. In his third year, he is diagnosed with testicular cancer.

1958–1959: Marty graduates from Harvard Law School. In 1958 Ruth transfers to Columbia University School of Law when Marty gets a job in New York City. She graduates, tied for first in her class.

1959–1961: Ruth works as a law clerk for Judge Edmund L. Palmieri, of the U.S. District Court for the Southern District of New York.

1961–1963: Ruth travels to Sweden to study the Swedish judicial system and learns the Swedish language to do this.

1961: President John F. Kennedy creates the Commission on the Status of Women.

June 10, 1963: Congress passes the Equal Pay Act, which states that women must receive the same pay as men for doing the same work.

1963–1972: By 1970 Ruth is a full professor of law with tenure at Rutgers Law School, State University of New Jersey. She is only the second woman to teach full-time at Rutgers.

1964: Title VII of the Civil Rights Act of 1964 makes it illegal to discriminate on the basis of sex in employment.

1965: Ruth publishes *Civil Procedure in Sweden*, with Anders Bruzelius.

September 8, 1965: James Steven Ginsburg is born.

1967: President Lyndon Johnson's executive order forbids sex discrimination by any government or recipient of government contracts.

June 25, 1971: Ruth co-writes her first brief for the U.S. Supreme Court in *Reed v. Reed*, 404 US 71, 1971.

January 1972: Ruth leaves Rutgers to become the first tenured woman professor at Columbia Law School.

1972: Title IX is passed. This measure prohibits sex discrimination in any federally funded educational program, including academic and athletic programs.

Spring 1972–1980: Ruth co-founds the Women's Rights Project of the American Civil Liberties Union (ACLU). She argues six gender discrimination cases before the U.S. Supreme Court: *Frontiero v. Richardson* (1973); *Kahn v. Shevin* (1973); *Weinberger v. Wiesenfeld* (1974); *Edwards v. Healy* (1974); *Califano v. Goldfarb* (1976); and *Duren v. Missouri* (1978).

1980–1993: She serves on the U.S. Court of Appeals for the District of Columbia Circuit. Marty becomes a professor at Georgetown University Law Center.

1981: Sandra Day O'Connor is appointed as the first woman justice on the U.S. Supreme Court.

August 10, 1993: Ruth Bader Ginsburg becomes the 107th Supreme Court justice and the second woman to serve on the Court. On October 4, 1993, she begins her term.

1996: Ginsburg writes the majority opinion in *United States v. Virginia*, stating that qualified women cannot be denied admission to Virginia Military Institute.

1999: She is diagnosed with cancer but does not miss a day on the bench. In 2009 Ruth has a second bout with cancer.

June 27, 2010: Martin Ginsburg dies.

AUTHOR'S NOTE

As a child, I loved school and learning. I got high marks in school. I was a serious piano student from the time I was six years old. Once, I overheard my mother's friend warn her that I was too smart and talented for my own good, which really meant that it would be hard for me to "get" a husband. And that was the cherished goal for women then: fulfilling the traditional roles of wife and mother.

Perhaps I was luckier than most, because I went to a high school where teachers encouraged their students' talents regardless of their gender. I went to a college where the emphasis was on intellectual exploration. However, not one professor ever explained to my women friends or me about how the "real" world would respond to us because we were women. It was only in the 1970s when I joined a consciousness-raising group that I realized how damaging gender expectations were for both women and men, and how damaging they had been for me.

Ruth Bader Ginsburg's work in fighting for gender equality is therefore very personal for me. She has dedicated her life to the liberation of not only women, but also men. Her work and the work of other trailblazers has transformed lives. There's still much work left to do, but society has changed enough that my granddaughters never think that their dreams are limited because they are women.

ILLUSTRATOR'S NOTE

Recently, while I was visiting a school, a child asked me, "What is the best part of your job?" I answered, "The fact that I learn something with every book I illustrate." When I first read the remarkable manuscript Doreen Rappaport had written for this book, I was immediately amazed by the life and work of Ruth Bader Ginsburg. As I began the process of drawing the initial storyboard sketches and doing the necessary research, I was struck by how much I was learning not just about Ruth but also about the laws of this country. The most rewarding part of this project was having to read the Constitution of the United States of America in order to paint the cover of the book. While I painted, I slowly began to understand and accept the notion that "We the People" refers to all of us, the citizens of this country, as opposed to just the men who wrote the Constitution, and that the government and the laws of this country were designed to serve us all. It might sound simple, but this was huge for me. My hope with this book is that everyone will ultimately be compelled to read the Constitution and familiarize themselves with the Bill of Rights—and be inspired to uphold and further the work and legacy of Ruth Bader Ginsburg. Illustrating this book has been an honor.

SELECTED BIBLIOGRAPHY

Altschuler, Glenn C. and Isaac Kramnick. *Cornell: A History, 1940–2015*. Ithaca, N.Y.: Cornell University Press, 2014.

Ayer, Eleanor. *Ruth Bader Ginsburg: Fire and Steel on the Supreme Court*. New York: Dillon Press, 1994.

Carmon, Irin and Shana Knizhnik. *Notorious RBG: The Life and Times of Ruth Bader Ginsburg*. New York: Dey St., 2015.

"A Conversation with Justice Ruth Bader Ginsburg" (interview conducted by ABC correspondent Lynn Sherr). Reprinted in *The Record of the Association of the Bar of the City of New York*, Vol. 56, No. 1, Winter 2001.

Davidson, Amy. "Ruth Bader Ginsburg's Retirement Dissent." *The New Yorker*, September 24, 2014.

Dodson, Scott, ed. *The Legacy of Ruth Bader Ginsburg*. New York: Cambridge University Press, 2015.

Filipovic, Jill. "Justice Ginsburg's distant dream of an all-female supreme court." *The Guardian*, November 30, 2012.

Gilbert, Lynn and Gaylen Moore. *Particular Passions: Talks with Women Who Have Shaped Our Times*. New York: Crown Books, 1981.

Ginsburg, Ruth Bader. Letter to the author. 7 August 2017.

———. "Remarks on Women Becoming Part of the Constitution." *Law and Inequality: A Journal of Theory and Practice*, Vol. 6, Issue 1, Article 4, 1988.

———. U.S. Supreme Court Justice Nomination Acceptance Address, delivered June 14, 1993, in the Rose Garden of the White House, Washington, D.C.

Ginsburg, Ruth with Mary Hartnett and Wendy W. Williams. *My Own Words*. New York: Simon & Schuster, 2016.

Halberstam, Malvina. "Ruth Bader Ginsburg: The First Jewish Woman on the United States Supreme Court," in *Jewish Women in America: An Historical Encyclopedia*, edited by Paula. E. Hyman and Deborah Dash Moore. New York: Routledge, 1997.

Hirshman, Linda. *Sisters in Law: How Sandra Day O'Connor and Ruth Bader Ginsburg Went to the Supreme Court and Changed the World*. New York: Harper, an imprint of HarperCollins Publishers, 2015.

Izadi, Elahe. "Ruth Bader Ginsburg's Advice on Love and Leaning In." *Washington Post*, July 31, 2014.

Liptak, Adam. "For a Collegial Court, Justices Lunch Together, and Forbid Talk of Cases." *New York Times*, June 1, 2016.

Margolick, David. "Trial by Adversity Shapes Jurist's Outlook." *New York Times*, June 25, 1993.

Rosen, Jeffrey. "Ruth Bader Ginsburg Is an American Hero." *The New Republic*, September 28, 2014.

Sacks, Mike. "Supreme Court Justice Ruth Bader Ginsburg Talks Constitution, Women and Liberty on Egyptian TV." *The Huffington Post*, February 1, 2012. huffingtonpost.com/2012/02/01/justice-ruth-bader-ginsburg-egypt_n_1248527.html.

Swiger, Elinor Porter. *Women Lawyers at Work*. New York: J. Messner, 1978.

Toobin, Jeffrey. "HEAVYWEIGHT: How Ruth Bader Ginsburg has moved the Supreme Court." *The New Yorker*, March 11, 2013.

———. "Will Ginsburg's Ledbetter Play Work Twice?" *The New Yorker*, June 24, 2013.

Weisberg, Jessica. "Supreme Court Justice Ruth Bader Ginsburg: 'I'm Not Going Anywhere.'" *Elle*, October 2014.

TO LEARN MORE ABOUT RUTH BADER GINSBURG, READ:

Bayer-Berenbaum, Linda. *Ruth Bader Ginsburg*. Philadelphia: Chelsea House Publishers, 2000.

Levy, Debbie. Illustrated by Elizabeth Baddeley. *I Dissent: Ruth Bader Ginsburg Makes Her Mark*. New York: Simon & Schuster, 2016.

Winter, Jonah. Illustrated by Stacy Innerst. *Ruth Bader Ginsburg: The Case of R.B.G. vs. Inequality*. New York: Abrams, 2017.

ACKNOWLEDGMENTS

I thank Laurel Eisner, Kate Andrias (a former law clerk of Ruth Bader Ginsburg), and Justice Ginsburg for their generosity of time and knowledge reading and critiquing my manuscript.

SOURCE NOTES

In many instances, quotes by Ruth Bader Ginsburg have been shortened without changing their meaning. Punctuation has been simplified. The text begins on page 6. The quote on the front endpapers comes from "A Conversation with Justice Ruth Bader Ginsburg." The quote on page 6 is from "Ruth Bader Ginsburg: The First Jewish Woman on the United States Supreme Court." The quotes on pages 8–9 are from *My Own Words* ("Nancy was an adventurer . . ."), *Notorious RBG: The Life and Times of Ruth Bader Ginsburg* ("an adventurer, who could think for herself . . ."), and *Sisters in Law: How Sandra Day O'Connor and Ruth Bader Ginsburg Went to the Supreme Court and Changed the World* ("My mother was the bravest . . ."). The quote on page 10 is from *Notorious RBG*. The quote on page 13 is from *My Own Words*. The quote on page 14 is from a letter to the author from Ruth Bader Ginsburg, dated August 7, 2017. The quote on page 16 is from *Sisters in Law*. The quotes on page 18 are from *Particular Passions: Talks with Women Who Have Shaped Our Times*. The quote on page 21 is from *Notorious RBG*. The quote on page 22 is from "Remarks on Women Becoming Part of the Constitution." The quote on page 24 is from "Trial by Adversity Shapes Jurist's Outlook." The quote on page 27 is from "Supreme Court Justice Ruth Bader Ginsburg: 'I'm Not Going Anywhere.'" The quote on page 28 is from "Trial by Adversity Shapes Jurist's Outlook." The quote on page 30 is from *Notorious RBG*. The quote on page 33 is from U.S. Supreme Court Justice Nomination Acceptance Speech ("I pray that I may be all . . ."). The quote on page 34 is from *Notorious RBG*. The quote on page 37 is from "Ruth Bader Ginsburg Is an American Hero." The quote on page 38 is from *My Own Words*. The quote on page 40 is from "Justice Ginsburg's distant dream of an all-female Supreme Court." The back endpaper quote is from "Supreme Court Justice Ruth Bader Ginsburg Talks Constitution, Women and Liberty on Egyptian TV."

"*I'm a very strong believer in listening and learning from others.*"